A Magic Mouse Guide

Internet

by
Chris Ward-Johnson
and the Magic Mouse

Illustrations & layout by
Laughing Gravy Design

Enslow Publishers, Inc.

40 Industrial Road	PO Box 38
Box 398	Aldershot
Berkeley Heights, NJ 07922	Hants GU12 6BP
USA	UK

http://www.enslow.com

Editor's note

Computers and software vary considerably. In this book we present information that is generally true of all computers and show a variety of particular screens. Do not worry if your screen is not the same as the one that appears in the book.

Acknowledgments

The publishers would like to thank the following for permission to use their photographs and copyright material:
Air India; Boeing; Eudora; Microsoft; Netscape.

In memory of Jonathan Inglis

Library of Congress Cataloging-in-Publication Data

Ward-Johnson, Chris.
      Internet : a magic mouse guide / Chris Ward-Johnson; illustrations & layout by Laughing Gravy Design.
            v. cm. — (Magic mouse guides)
      Includes index.
      Contents: The Internet — Internet service provider — on the Internet — World wide web — Addresses — Searching the net — Menus and downloading — E-mail — Chatting on the Internet — Newsgroups — Games — Safety on the net.
      ISBN 0-7660-2260-9 (hardcover)
      1. Internet—Juvenile literature. [1. Internet.] I. Laughing Gravy Design. II. Title. III. Series: Ward-Johnson, Chris. Magic mouse guides.
TK5105.875.I57.W377 2003
004.67'8—dc21

2002013274

Printed in Dubai by Oriental Press.

10 9 8 7 6 5 4 3 2 1

To Our Readers:

We have done our best to make sure all Internet addresses in this book were active and appropriate when we went to press. However, the author and the publisher have no control over and assume no liability for the material available on those Internet sites or on other Web sites they may link to. Any comments or suggestions can be sent by e-mail to comments@enslow.com or to the address on the backcover.

First published by Cherrytree Books
(a member of the Evans Publishing Group)
327 High Street, Slough, Berkshire SL1 1TX, UK
Copyright © Evans Brothers Limited 2001
This edition published under licence from Evans Brothers Limited
All rights reserved
Designed and produced by A S Publishing
Illustrations and layout by Gary Dillon & Phil Jolly at
Laughing Gravy Design

Contents

Mouse tips

Don't worry if your screen does not always look exactly like the ones in the book.

If there are words you don't understand, look on pages 28-31.

Mouse tips

3

The internet

Hari is going to India for his vacation. His best friend Ben is upset. Who will he play with?

"Don't worry!" says Hari. "We can keep in touch through the internet."

The internet is a giant collection of
computers all over the world.
Anyone who has a computer connected
to the internet can talk to anyone else
who is connected.

The computers are linked by a huge
network of cables and satellites.

Many people call
the internet the
"net"
for short.

Internet service provider

To use the internet, you need a computer, a modem and an internet service provider, or ISP.

An internet service provider provides you with the software programs you need and links you to the internet.

If you are linked by a regular telephone line, you have to pay each time you are connected.

ISP

Modem

There is lots of information you can share on the net. Once you know how, you can see pictures and read books and play games on the net.

Ben's sister Liza shows Ben how to find out about Mumbai, India, where Hari is going to stay with his uncle.

You can tell when some modems are connecting to the telephone. They sound like a mouse. When you are connected, you are online.

On the internet

The next day, Ben goes online. He finds an article about Mumbai in an encyclopedia on the world wide web. Then he watches part of a film about the city. There are crowds of people in the streets. They wear very bright clothes. He listens to a live radio show from Mumbai.

Moving from one page of the web to another is called browsing or surfing the net. To browse the net Ben uses a software program called a web browser. He looks up pages on the world wide web. One page leads him on to another through a hyperlink.

Most browsers have a home page and a Back and Forward button. You can click on them to move through the pages or return to the start.

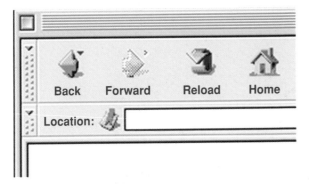

Back   Forward   Reload   Home

Location:

Ask before you go online. It can cost lots of money if you stay online for a long time.

9

World wide web

The world wide web is like a great big book with millions of pages. Many of these pages have color, sound and moving pictures.

The pages are called websites, or sites for short. Anyone can have a website. They can put information about themselves on the site. Companies have websites that tell people about the products they make.

WWW

Everyone with a website has an address.
Hari gives Ben the address of his uncle's
website in Mumbai. He gives him his
e-mail address too. Ben and Liza go to
the airport with Hari to say goodbye.

"Goodbye, Hari. Have a good time!"

You can store
website addresses
you use a lot in your
Bookmarks or
Favorites.

Addresses

To look up a website you have to type in its internet address. Internet addresses are called URLs. This stands for uniform resource locators.

Web addresses look like this:

http://www.airindia.com

The first group of letters tells the net which protocol to use. A protocol is like a language.

The second group is the domain address: www stands for world wide web.

airindia stands for Air India.

The last word tells you what kind of site it is. Air India is a company.

Always copy addresses exactly. Do not leave spaces.

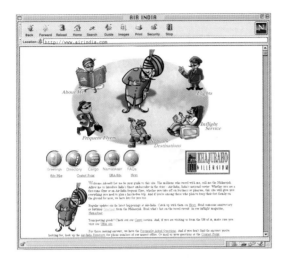

When you type an address you must get every word or symbol just right.

http stands for hypertext transfer protocol. After it comes a colon and two slashes.

Searching the net

You do not have to know the address to find a website. Your web browser will help you find it.

Ben wants to find out about the plane Hari is flying on. He uses a search engine. This tells him to type in what he wants to find in a search box. He types in "Boeing 747." A long list of pages appears on the screen. Ben chooses one and clicks on it. It does not have any pictures, so he clicks on the hyperlink. This takes him to another page.

Boeing 747 profile

Follow the search instructions carefully. Be as clear as you can. Use Help to help you.

14

Search

This time there are pictures and lots of information.

Menus and downloading

Some search services give you a menu to choose from. Each menu gives you a narrower choice. Ben clicks on India, then on Mumbai, then on the name of the street that Hari's uncle lives in. He finds the name of the shop and looks at the website.

Rajiv Desai
COMPUTERS

Ben wants to keep the pages he has downloaded. The computer asks him if he wants to Save the file and he clicks on OK. Once it is saved, Ben prints out the pages on his printer.

You cannot always download files. For some you need a password or you need to pay for them.

17

E-mail

The next day Ben gets an e-mail from Hari.

```
Dear Ben
Terrific flight. The food was super. Uncle
Rajiv has a huge computer network. It links
his factory, his warehouse, his shops, and
his house. All the workers can get informa-
tion from it. It even prints his bills. There
are ten computers in one room. It's great.

Bye,
Hari.
```

E-mail is like sending a letter by phone. You can send words, pictures, sounds and even videos by e-mail.

Your internet service provider gives you a software program and an e-mail address. A pretend e-mail address might look like this:

suzymouse@mouseville.com

The first part of the address is the name of the person or company. The @ sign means "at." The next part is the name of the ISP or server. The next part tells you what kind of a place it is.

You do not have to leave your computer on to get e-mails. Your ISP keeps them until you ask for them.

Chatting on the internet

Ben sends Hari an e-mail and gives him the address of a chat room. Now he and Hari can "talk" to each other directly. They can type messages and read the replies on screen.

You can talk to all sorts of people in chat rooms. But you must always ask a grown-up before you use one. Hari's uncle says Hari can talk to Ben but he must not give anyone his real name or address. And he must not talk for long.

Remember NEVER to give your real name, address or telephone number to anyone on the internet. Some very odd people use chat rooms.

Talking on the internet is cheaper than talking on the telephone. But it still costs money.

Newsgroups

Ben keeps asking Hari questions about baseball in India. Hari does not always know the answers.

Liza suggests that they join a newsgroup. Their parents say they can, but they must remember not to give their addresses or phone numbers. Hari's uncle says they can too but they must not stay online too long.

Ben and Hari use a program called a newsreader that comes with their internet browser. It lets them choose from thousands of newsgroups.

Baseball

Newsgroups are like giant bulletin boards. Each one has a theme. You might want to join one about horseback riding or about math. Ben and Hari join one about baseball.

Anybody in the newsgroup can ask a question or answer one. Anyone can write an article about the subject. Everyone can join in discussions.

You do not have to pay to join a newsgroup. But it still takes time and costs money to use the net.

Games

Suddenly Hari is not there anymore. He has gone on a trip with his uncle and aunt. Day after day Ben has to play on his own. He decides to play a new game on his computer. He finds a games newsgroup and joins it. He learns how to download a program that lets him play chess with a boy in France.

Next he plays a fantasy game of Dungeons and Dragons with several other people. He plays a dragon but gets beaten by a slimy toad.

24

Then he tries out some new games but he cannot download them without paying. His mom says he can't do it right now.

Instead Ben downloads some theme tunes from his favorite television programs. They are free. He plays them loudly on his computer.

You can try out lots of things for free on the internet. A good place to look is at:

http://shareware.cnet.com

You can get a free picture of your favorite celebrity.

25

Safety on the net

At last Hari is home from Mumbai. He brings a jade elephant for Liza and some mangoes for Ben. He tells them all about the people he met and the places he saw.

He sends an e-mail to his uncle and aunt.

Thank you for a wonderful vacation. I hope
your computer did not get a virus. Being
online was great but not as cool as seeing
the real Mumbai. And you were right. Sometimes
the net is very slow.

I will keep my promises. I will never give my
name, address or phone number to anyone. I
won't go online without asking and I won't
surf all the time.

And I promise to come back to Mumbai if you ask
me again. My friend Ben would like to come too.

Love from Hari.

More about the internet

Address Everyone on the internet has an address that enables any other user to find them. Each address begins with a set of characters that tells the internet what protocol or "language" you are using.

Alta Vista A popular search engine.

Bookmarks A list you can keep on your computer of web pages that you use a lot.

Browser Software that helps you find your way around the internet.

Chat room Place on the net where you can have conversations with other net users.

Domain Part of an internet address that says where the computer is. The first part is the user name, for example, magic-mouse. The next part tells where the user is, for example, in a college (edu) or business (com).

Download When a page from the web or an e-mail message is copied from the internet to your computer, it downloads.

E-mail Electronic mail.

Favorites A list you can keep on your computer of web pages that you use a lot.

Games You can download many games from the net. To play games online with other people you need special software.

Google A popular search engine.

http Short for hypertext transfer protocol.

Hyperlink In a hypertext document there are certain icons and words, usually in color and underlined, that are linked to other pages. If you select one of these and click on it a new page appears.

Hypertext transfer protocol The "language'" used to link and transfer hypertext documents on the internet.

Internet A worldwide network of millions of linked computers.

Internet service provider A company that you pay to provide you with a link to the internet.

ISP Short for internet service provider.

Microsoft Internet Explorer A popular web browser.

Menu A list of commands that gives you a choice of what to do next. Some choices open up dialog boxes.

Modem A device that links a computer to a telephone line and enables the user to send faxes and e-mails and gain access to the internet.

Net Short for internet.

Netscape A popular web browser.

Newsgroups A place where people with the same interest can read, write and exchange news and views.

Newsreader Software program that enables you to take part in a newsgroup.

Online You are online whenever you are connected to the internet. It is cheaper to read messages and information downloaded from the net when you are offline.

Password Set of characters that you can key into your computer to let your service provider know that it is you and not somebody else using your computer.

Payment Using the internet costs money. You have to pay the service provider to connect you, and sometimes you have to pay the telephone company for the time spent online. If you download software, games or magazines you usually have to pay for them too. Often you can pay by credit card. Always ask for permission before you go online or if you want to buy something on the internet.

Printing You can print out many pages from the internet without payment but sometimes you have to pay. Printing out pages with pictures usually takes a long time and uses lots of memory.

Program A set of electronic instructions that tell your computer what to do.

Protocol A kind of language with special rules that computers use to communicate on the internet.

Safety The internet can be a dangerous place. Many odd people use it and try to trick nice people into meeting them or giving them money. Follow these rules to keep safe.

- Never go online without asking permission.

- Never tell anyone where you live or where you go to school.

- Never give anyone your phone number.

- Never give anyone your password.

- Never arrange to meet anyone you do not already know.

- Never meet anyone without asking your parents first.

- If anything on the internet makes you feel uncomfortable or upset, tell your parents or your teacher.

Satellite A gadget that orbits the earth and relays information and electronic messages to different places on earth. The internet uses satellites to link computers all around the world.

Search box Where you type the address of a website you want to visit.

Search engine A program that helps you find information on the internet. Google, Yahoo! and Alta Vista are popular search engines.

Site Short for website.

Software Computer programs that you can use for various purposes, such as browsing the web, using newsgroups or sending e-mails.

Sound You can download sounds or music from the internet if you have the right programs and equipment.

Surfing Going from one web page to another and seeing what you find.

Uniform resource locator The way each address is written on the internet so that anyone can find it.

URL Short for uniform resource locator.

Virus A program designed to interfere with other programs. When you download a program from the internet it may contain a hidden virus that will harm your files. You can get software that will search programs for viruses.

Web address A sequence of words and symbols that enables internet users to find each page of the world wide web. It is also called a uniform resource locator, or URL.

Web browser Software that helps you find your way round the world wide web on the internet. Netscape and Microsoft Internet Explorer are the two most popular.

Web page Another name for a website.

Website Any one of billions of documents, or web pages, each with its own address on the world wide web.

World wide web Collection of pages, or sites, on the internet that anyone with the right equipment can see. They may contain pictures, sounds, cartoons and videos. The pages are written in hypertext so that users can move easily from one page to another by means of hyperlinks.

www Short for world wide web.

Yahoo! A popular search engine.

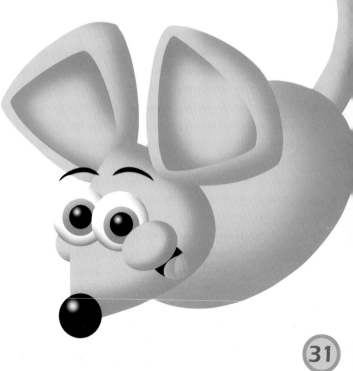

Index